FOREPLAY:

Sexual Healing for Spiritual Wholeness

FOREPLAY:

Sexual Healing for Spiritual Wholeness

by Jamal-Harrison Bryant

Published by
GREENPOPE Publishing
Baltimore, Maryland

Printed in the United States of America

FIRST EDITION – May 2002

Creative Direction: Jamal-Harrison Bryant
Edited by: Sharon Page
Book Design: Jamal-Harrison Bryant & Eric Oliver

Library of Congress Catalog Card Number: 2002102247

ISBN: 0-9718700-0-4

USA $15
Canada $17.50

DEDICATION

This book was birthed out of a lot of love.

To my heavenly father who sent PERFECT love through his son Jesus.

To my parents who gave UNCONDITIONAL love when I was unbearable.

To my daughter, Topaz, who gives PURE love..... especially when we're going to Chuck E. Cheese's.

To the members of Empowerment Temple, who express CONSISTENT love as I develop as a pastor and leader.

To Sharon Page and Pamela Crockett for SISTERLY love to see and push the potential of my possibilities in order to get this book done.

and last but not least ....

To Lady Gizelle who GOD sent me to show me TRUE love.

To anybody that I forgot to mention I got nothing but LOVE for ya !

CONTENTS

INTRODUCTION

This is a testament to my own spiritual development and deliverance. One of the invisible enemies to the society of the saved is sexuality. The illicit spirit of fornication runs rampant in many congregations and adultery seems to be the norm around the country. I can attest at 30 years of age, I've never touched a cigarette or tasted alcohol. However, the area of my life that had me bound was an affliction of my flesh that led to sordid sexual escapades. I grew up in the church, third generation minister, was in a nurturing healthy environment, however none of that gave me the discipline to protect my physical temple from fleshly impulses.

I went on all the retreats; attended all the conferences; listened to all the tapes; heard all the sermons; but the themes of "JUST SAY NO"; "LEARNING TO WAIT"; and "ABSTINENCE IS THE ANSWER" never seemed to resonate. Just like the prodigal son who spent all that he had on riotous living and women, I didn't come to myself until I woke up in a pig-pen with mud on my face. Albeit a stony journey to finally reach the conclusion that it was time for me to go home to holiness. It took becoming a single father; a gold patron for the termination of unwanted pregnancies; almost losing the woman whose love I took for granted; being an unofficial travel agent for imported flights of fancy; unknowingly looking like a clown for trying to juggle people instead of balls; and transforming into Inspector Gadget in a futile attempt to keep my sins from being discovered. All the while professing to be saved and a servant.

It merits to mention that every woman whom I've ever been involved with was also "saved" thereby revealing that the enslavement to sexuality was a demonic equal opportunity destroyer. I've come to discern that sexuality amongst the saved isn't a habit, it's a spirit that must be conquered and destroyed! An entire generation could very easily be lost from the kingdom, if we continue to put band-aids in areas that require open-heart surgery.

This book is an adaptation from a series that I preached at the most powerful place on the planet -- which happens to be the church I'm blessed enough to pastor -- Empowerment Temple A.M.E. in Baltimore, Maryland. It was after this series that our ministry really began to take off and skyrocket. There was a clear indication that there were many like me who knew they were spiritually out of sync and in need of a relational, psychological and emotional adjustment. It's my prayer that this book helps you begin your journey towards healing and deliverance. For this is simple Foreplay: SEXUAL HEALING FOR SPIRITUAL WHOLENESS. Penetration won't happen until YOU make up your mind that you're willing to go all the way with GOD!

I NEED SOME FOREPLAY

The untimely dismissal of Tavis Smiley from BET uncovered and exposed many of the problems and concerns that African-Americans have had with BET for over 20 years. It brought to light the curators of American culture who have attempted, since "Birth of a Nation", to depict black love not as something that is sensual, but rather and instead something that is barbaric.

Given the nine hours of crude videos and ignorant comedians that bombard our television sets on any given day, it has sent a poor signal to misguided young black men who feel that the depth of touching a black woman's sensuality is covered in platinum or a Bentley and chrome rims. They see every day our black women sitting on the hoods of cars with bikinis on or less. And there is not any intonation towards intimacy, but rather an alien encounter by which they never get to know one another for whom they are or under the banner of a Christian guided relationship.

You will note that many of our black men have found as the blueprint for romanticism Jay-Z's "Give It to Me." You've asked and heard Missy Elliott's "Is That Your Chick?" You've heard them sing "Get Crunked Up." But none of them deal with romancing the mind and the spirit and the whole being of somebody's personhood in their complete totality. So I would dare say that we cannot then simply pin or place blame on what white America has done to us but rather and instead what it is that we have done to ourselves.

We have made it common fare to call the women we love female dogs and farming equipment, with no accountability or responsibility for nurturing them in the bare essence of their soul and their womanhood. It is then a foreign asterisk, lost in the annals of time, to find on television some black man opening the door for a black woman; or to witness a brother treating a sister with dignity and respect. In fact, now that we have found ourselves in a hip hop/gangster rap mentality we see behavior that is barbaric where we ought to operate out of intimacy. And so many of us have not been able to decipher and discern the distinction between an intimate relationship and an alien relationship.

An intimate relationship can be defined as one whereby you are close to someone within the privacy of their own personal space. On the reverse, an alien relationship is simply when you roll up out of bed and you don't even know that person's last name, where they live, or who and where their mama is.

So many of us call ourselves Christians, yet base our realities and our relationships in a lost ark mentality where, in fact, we are seekers and destroyers of flesh and not dealing with the fact that God has called upon and for us to have an intimate relationship.

You cannot have an intimate relationship with somebody who you do not know. The most precious and most private thing that you possess is your sexuality. But when you give your sexuality away wholesale that is in fact sending a signal that you no longer respect or value yourself.

I visited Atlanta not long ago, and went into a department store downtown by the name of Friedman Shoes. When I was going into Friedman Shoes, I saw a pair of shoes that I wanted in the window display. I went upstairs and asked the shoe sales clerk to please give me that particular pair of shoes in a size 12. He brought the pair of shoes out and I did not recognize them. I said "no, I want the pair of shoes that are in the window." He said "Sir, these are the exact same pair of shoes." I said "these can't possibly be the same kind of shoes because they don't have the same color, they don't have the same fit, and they are not the same shape." He said "Sir the problem is they are the exact same pair of shoes but many people have tried these on; and the constant trying them on has caused them to lose their color, as well as their shape, and form." I then thought, the same thing is going to happen when God comes back for His children. He is going to say, "you are not the person that I ordained you to be and the reason why that you don't look like the person I created is because you've allowed too many people to try you on. Therefore you've lost your color, you've lost your shape and you've lost your form."

You have to understand that there is, in fact, a dynamic that we cannot ignore. Too many of us like to deal with sexuality while ignoring sensuality. Your sexuality then is based and immersed in your sensuality. Your sexuality is activation while your sensuality is motivation. Now, you become a sexual creature before you ever commit the act based on your sensual organs. What am I saying? You are sexual not just by your sexual organs but by your sensual glands because you have five areas of sensuality. What it is that you see, what it is that you touch, what it is that you hear, what it is that you feel, and what it is that you taste. In other words, what it is that you see sensually will prompt you to go into a sexual order.

Many of you need to understand that you commit sin not just by actions but also by your thoughts. Many of you have already committed a sin and experienced multiple orgasms of adultery and fornication sitting right in church, with somebody whom you've never met, and who's name you don't even know! That is so because the Bible says "so as a man thinketh, so is he." So even when you think you're sitting idle, you may have to clean it up.

To further elaborate, you have to understand that you are sensual before you are sexual because your sexual drive is prompted, first of all, by what it is that you see. Then once you see it, you get in your mind "I want it." But then if you touch it, you've moved even further into the twilight zone because now you've "got to have it." But more than that, if you can touch it and you see it, it occupies your space. Many of you understand that this is a realm of sensuality that you may not be able to handle because it will inevitably lead you to sexuality. You know that there is a certain place you just can't handle to be touched. "Oh God, if you have a secret don't whisper in my ear. You better write it down!" That is a clear and familiar example of how your sensuality will parlay you into your sexuality.

Now for some people who are saved and have been removed from sexual activity for a long time it is easier to stay saved, because you don't even remember. But others just have to close themselves in.

Temptation is tougher the closer you are to it. The first seven days is usually the most gruesome. Your mind is doing laps around a cesspool. You start making cameo appearances in the editors cut of "Sleepless In Seattle." Songs and shows trigger untapped emotions. That's why when you ask for space you're asking for space and time to get yourself together and to protect your sexuality. If you can get past the first week the additional weeks become a little bit easier, not to say that it's not difficult.

Now for the women who are contemplating or are on the verge of marriage, you need to marry someone who can take care of you because you understand that when you marry, the man that you marry ought to take you to the next level. There is no reason for you to get married and still be broke. The role of the man is to take you to another place. In other words then, when you get married, you ought to dress better. You ought to drive better. You ought to live better. And you ought to eat better. I'm sure many of your grandmothers have said just like mine "I can do bad all by myself!"

The objective of course would be to find a Christian man, who has a job. But many of you sisters need to understand how to get him because you can't just step to him any kind of way. You have to make sure that you stand out above the crowd. This is what I need you to do. First of all, make sure your relationship with the Lord is strong and growing. The next thing I need you to do is make sure that you are presentable. Working from the inside out, your presentation should be representative of both who you are and whom you seek. The third thing that you may want to do is spray on an appealing scent. Because before you are sexual, you are sensual. Not only that, remember that your appearance does matter. It is a reflection of how you see yourself. Don't be trying to find no man with no run over heels on! And after you've done all of that, then what I need you to do is let the Holy Spirit take control.

I want you to just trust God and wait. I need you to wait because you don't need to go after him. He's going to come after you because after he sees and smells you and knows that you're in his presence, he's going to want to know who you are! I know there's somebody reading this book who has been chasing after some Negro. God said "just sit still and wait on me to do it!"

You can't be too forward and too aggressive trying to jump in bed with the man you seek or think you've found. Take your time, because if you rush to get in the bed, he's going to roll over and not respect you in the morning. But if he sees that you are dressed with quality, that you smell like you are somebody, that you look like you're doing alright without him, then that will attract the right attention from him. He'll have no choice but to give you his attention. Sisters, stop looking so needy climbing into bed trying to get a man.

Now I know you can't believe this is in the Bible. It's right in the book of Ruth. God woke me up in the middle of the night and said, "exactly what Naomi told Ruth to do is the same thing that I want them to do for me." God is so sick of saints coming to Him trying to get a quickie and never romancing Him for who He is. You go to church screaming, shouting and hollering. But you have not been intimate with God all week long! Stop trying to treat God like a sugar daddy and start romancing God saying, "I'm yours Lord. Everything I got, everything I'm not!"

Let's see if these principles will in fact carry over because the God we serve, which is the God of love, demands and requires of us foreplay before He gives us what we need. In the book of Ruth, the mother-in-law tells Ruth, "you have to wash." I found somewhere in John that "I am cleansed by the word of God." Brothers and sisters you don't understand that when you sit in the gospel of Jesus Christ, you are taking a shower. When you hear the punctuated, unadulterated word of God; then the dirt and grime that you've accumulated all week long begins to wash off of you. I'm tired of all the dirt I had to go through. My name was dragged through the mud. My reputation has been ripped apart, and so I'm standing in the word. You have to ask God to "create in you a clean heart and renew a right spirit." Stand in the word. Then wait upon the Lord to renew strength.

Not only are you cleansed by the word, but by the same token, Naomi tells Ruth to put on expensive perfume because she understood the correlation between sensuality and sexuality. She said in essence, if you motivate his sense of smell, then it will activate his response. Some of you are saying, "I do not understand where it is that I can get a perfume that will get God's attention." No, I'm not talking about Issey Miyake. This is not a job for Givago. This is not a job for Gucci Rush. But if you go to Corinthians it says that I put on the "aroma of Christ." Now I know that we've been brought up and taught to believe that we ought to walk like Jesus. We ought to talk like Jesus. We ought to live like Jesus. But nobody ever told you to smell like Jesus. Now some of you have to understand that you smell like Jesus when you have the anointing.

The perfume gives two different and distinct aromas. It does two things. The first thing that it does is it repels the enemy. Some folks can sniff out that you're saved and that's why they won't mess with you. Because they know that there is something about you, that you are not going to stand for any foolishness. The second thing that it does is it brings a blessing to you because the angels descend when they smell you, because they know that Jesus is close by.

Now some of us put on too much of the wrong stuff. But there's something about when you are sprayed with the anointing of God that stuff that should've driven you crazy; you don't even lose sleep about it anymore. This is what I found out. Sometimes you have to understand what anointed perfume does. I found out that some prayers will not change people. No matter how long you pray for them, they are going to stay the same. They were born mean, they're living mean, and they're going to die mean. But then I also found that no matter how much you pray, sometimes God won't change situations. No matter how much you pray you're going to stay in the hood. You're going to keep driving that hooptie. But what I found that prayer does, sometimes prayer may not change people or situations, but it'll change how you look at people and how you look at situations! Because you used to give people too much power and authority over your life.

The third thing that Naomi tells Ruth is to put on your best outfit. God said, "if you really want to turn me on, if you really want to get my attention put on that little thing I bought you." "What are you talking about God?" You know that thing that I picked you up in Ephesians –"the whole armor of God. Put on the breastplate of righteousness, the shield of faith, the sword of the spirit." I may not look like nothing to you but I have on the whole armor of God.

In Ruth, Boaz said, "I appreciate you because you waited on me." God is saying, you had other opportunities to be with Negroes who are not saved but because you walked away from stuff that could have given you a rise for the moment and said, "I'll wait on God," because you were "faithful over a few things I'm now going to make you ruler over many." Now some of you have never waited on God before.

Boaz told Ruth, "bring me your shawl." He put barley in the shawl because he understood as a good provider that he had to give her resources after he slept with her. (That just went over your head.) Now, some of you have had one-night stands where you left empty. But God said, "if you just sit at my feet. Just for sitting at my feet I'm going to give you so much stuff that you will not have room enough to receive – pressed down, shakin' together, running over."

You are trying to figure out why you are driving what you drive, how you are eating what you eat, how you are living where you live. It's because you woke up. Even when you thought about sleeping in the bed. Even when you forgot to turn your clock forward. God said, "because you rush to get to church on Sunday mornings I'm going to bless you with the desires of your heart."

Some of you have found that when you slept with other folk, it messed up your reputation. But when you sleep with God, it restores a bad reputation. And not only does it restore your reputation, He won't let you go until He finishes blessing you.

When you look back over your life, and you think about what God has done for you and see how He's elevated you and see how He's made a way for you, I just have one question, "Was He Good? Did He handle His business?!" You can't find a better sleeping partner.

What it is that you need from God may not manifest today. But if you keep praying and meditating and worshipping, before you know it, everything that you've been needing God to do He's going to do it. God has something wonderful for you! If you just learn to turn HIM on! And if you want to get God's attention, you better praise God like you need Him. You better yell like you know He's able. There is a prerequisite to being blessed. You can't jump in the church asking God to do stuff for you when you haven't done anything for Him. God said this is a two-way operation. If you need God to turn you out, you must turn him on!

Scriptural references - *Ruth 3:1-4.*   One day Naomi her mother-in-law said to her, "My daughter, should I not try to find a home for you, where you will be well provided for? Is not Boaz, with whose servant girls you have been a kinsman of ours? Tonight he will be winnowing barley on the threshing floor. Wash and perfume yourself and put on your best clothes. Then go down to the threshing floor, but don't let him know you are there until he has finished eating and drinking."

HANDLING HANNIBAL

A serious work as a contribution to the intellectual development of oppressed people in America, known as African-Americans, was scribed by a man by the name of Carter G. Woodson, who declared in no uncertain terms that there was (and is) a "Miseducation of the Negro." If we were to do a millennium reprint, we would have to suggest that there is a miseducation of America. Because America has done a job on miseducating our children. For instance, how do we celebrate Columbus as the discoverer of America while acknowledging when he arrived there was a welcoming committee who met him on the shore? The same and similar instance is true when you deal with entertainment, confusing and convoluting it with education.

You ought to understand that Hannibal was in fact an African warrior who was a defender of the Carthaginian people. He was able to single-handedly fight off the entire Roman Empire. He in fact faced the Alps Mountains and declared forthrightly in a voice of faith "Behold there are no Alps." He was a fighter and a defender. And then within recent vintage, because of the miseducation of America they transformed Hannibal from a defender into a devourer and gave him the name.... Hannibal Lector.

We have to then consider for ourselves how is it that a Black man who originated as a defender of life through an American lens is transformed into a devourer of life. And so for our children who have not been properly educated, when they hear then the name Hannibal, they automatically associate it with somebody who is a devourer and not somebody who is a defender.

We find ourselves then caught in a warp with sociological synonyms where it has the same name but has different meanings. For so many sisters then, when they hear the word "man", although God created man to be a defender, (because of their life experiences), they only know man as a devourer. So when they hear that there is a man, they will in fact give a universal umbrella that all men are dogs, because their limited experience show all men as devourers and not defenders.

How then do we misconstrue what it is that God has created. God has created the Black man to be a defender but through the lens of America he is transformed into a devourer? But I don't want to be so sociological that I'm remiss in being theological. When you then deal with the word Christian you find a warped meaning. A duality of purpose. There are some Christians who are defenders of the faith, but then there are other Christians that are devourers of the faith. These Christians don't stand up for God, but fall for anything that comes their way. There are some of you with people in your house, who are not saved, and are not sure whether or not to call you a Christian because they're not sure whether you are the Christian that God talks about in the Bible, or whether you are the Christian that they found out about in the social hall.

When in fact you cannot defend who you are, whether or not

you are a defender or a devourer, I think you have found yourself in the vice grip of the devil's claws. The devil wants to transform you from your original purpose, which is to defend life and take you into a lower stratum where you are the taker of life.

Now, if you understand that Jesus came so that you "might have life and have it more abundantly" and you smoke and know that smoking causes cancer, I think God says, "Why must you live when you're sending a smoke signal that you want to die?" If in fact you know that drinking will erode your liver and your father and grandfather died from drinking and you say that you are a casual drinker when you know that there is a generational curse that is, afflicted in your cells and DNA membrane, you are saying to God "I don't want to live, but I'd rather die."

Now, what you have to consider in the new millennium is "Are you a defender or are you a devourer?" Am I something that protects life or am I something that snatches life? And there are so many people out there who are tossed between two opinions. They don't know whether or not to give or take. Even though they cannot give or take! All they can do is preserve life, because God is the giver and the taker of all life. So what right does anyone have to tell you who you are going to be, when God created you to tell you who you are going to be?

For a fresh prospective on your lifestyle; I recommend that you consider "Hannibal".....the cinematic presentation. You will understand that there was something strange in the cinematic presentation of

Hannibal. I don't know how many of you are so saved that you don't go to the movies but when you look at this movie called "Hannibal" (which is the second sequel after "Silence of the Lambs") we find somebody twisted and deranged, yet intelligent. The female protagonist is an attorney by the name of Clarise. Clarise finds herself in Italy looking for somebody who tried to take her life. It says she went clear across the country trying to find him. Listen, when God gives you a way out of a situation, don't crawl back in, walk out and don't look back! Now what God dropped in my spirit is sometimes we chase after that which God has delivered us from. God released that person from you and you say you're just calling to see how they're doing. Hang the phone up!

Now if you understand that there is a diabolical and demonic scheme to take you out of your sanity and your life, you then clearly understand that there are some imps that have been assigned to you by name." There are some people that the devil keeps putting in your path and whenever you feel good, they try to make you feel bad. Have you not found that there is a family member in your house that every time you get a raise, every time you get a promotion, every time you get your life back together, they start "hating on you" declaring "You ain't all of that!" Say to them, baby don't be jealous, what God did for me, He'll double it for you!

Understand that your enemies come after you to devour your flesh. You must understand that satan is smart and not only is he smart, he is insightful. You might as well put on your life jacket. Because he knows that once you got saved, you bought an insurance policy for your soul. And because you bought an insurance policy for your soul, nobody can touch your soul. And because he can't touch your soul, he'll go after your body. What the devil tries to do is get through your body to contaminate your soul and infiltrate your mind. So the greatest threat against you is your flesh. The devil understands that the more your anointing increases the more your sexual drive increases.

You'll find the same man named David. Before he got anointed he was in the backyard mowing the lawn. But when God anointed him to be king, I bet he found himself in all kinds of sexual affairs. Now the problem with the church is that the church tries to neuter you to become asexual and try to act like you don't have the drive, the proclivities and the feelings that you feel. And then they try to send you off like you just ran away from a monastery and you don't know what it feels like.

The Bible says that satan came after his flesh. You have to understand that he comes after your flesh because if he gets to your flesh, then he can mess with your spirit. When the devil gets a hold of your body, he has a leasing agreement with your mind! In other words, there are some people reading this book, your body is there but your mind is on the other side of town! And you can't think about what it is that God has done for your spirit because you just remembered what happened to your body.

You remember a man by the name of Job? Job lost all of his

material things. His material things were an expression of him. He in fact said that when he lost his things that, "The Lord giveth and the Lord taketh away." But when the Lord let the devil touch his body, when he shaved his head, sat on an ash heap and began to curse the day he was born, it was at that point that his body got touched. His wife showed up and said "why don't you curse God and die."

Let me see if I can give a practical analysis. If in fact you're sleeping with somebody and you woke up the next morning and they stole some money out of your purse. You'll just chalk it up as a lost and say that person's a thief. But if you're sleeping with a person and you don't hear from them for two weeks, then they didn't steal some "thing" from you, they stole you! And because they stole you, you begin to think because intimacy is part of your spiritual nature that you don't want your self to be stolen.

But the problem with some of us is that we try to reconcile that after we are saved that we are no longer sexual. That's a lie! The problem with some of us is that we haven't come to terms with our sexuality in terms of our spirituality. The problem with us is that we have been conditioned that whatever it is that we feel in our internal nature, we equate it to sexuality when oft times it's spirituality. And so we call Jesus our husband because we have supernatural orgasms thinking that the move of the spirit is something sexual when we have not equated it to something spiritual. I think I better go a little bit further. A lot of you are attracted to your pastor, and you don't even know why. It's not because of your pastor himself, but because of the spirit that is in your pastor.

That's why it's hard to be saved and asexual because you have never been challenged to redirect your sexual energy into spiritual energy. God has to transform your thinking to understand that your body is not your own. Your body is a living sanctuary, pure and holy, tried and true.

You have to understand how is it that you can put your sexuality under submission to your spirituality. For those of you who saw "Silence of the Lambs," once they captured Hannibal, the first thing they had to do was muzzle his mouth, because the devil will talk you into anything. Many of you out there understand there's one person in the sphere of your life, if they call you one in the morning or three in the afternoon, you don't know what it is but you'll leave your job, you'll even leave the chicken in the oven. But it's something about hearing their voice. But there are some of you who have learned how to shut the devil up and say if God be for me what in the world can be against me. You better just tell the devil, "talk to the hand." That's why God has given you the gift of caller ID because sometimes you better not answer the phone. Sometimes you better not answer the door because you know what they want.

Now back to Hannibal, not only do they put a muzzle on his mouth, but you'll note that after they captured Hannibal, the second thing they did was handcuff his hands. They had to handcuff his hands because they knew if Hannibal ever put his hands on them that they wouldn't survive.

Now there is something metaphysical to the spiritual being that you want to be touched. You want to be touched and that's why the old church used to sing "He Touched Me." But because so many people touch you during the course of the week, when you feel the hand of God you don't recognize it because there has been so many hands on you. That's why I don't let everybody lay hands on me. Act like you're going to give somebody a high five then take it back and say don't touch me!

And sometimes you have to disarm your adversary so you are no longer in hands reach of the folk who are meaning to do you evil. The reality is, because God has given you a poised sense of discernment, you know the people who are after you just for your body, and are not interested in your mind and cannot help cultivate your spirit. You have to act like it's Hammer-time "You Can't Touch This!"

You have to understand that if God touches me, I don't need you to hold my hand. I don't need no holy hug. I don't need you to check to see if I'm all right because I'm going to be alright. Nobody said that the road was going to be easy, but I don't believe He brought me this far to leave me!

In the first case you handle Hannibal by putting a muzzle on his mouth. In the second case you handcuff his hands. And there are some people reading this book who have found what Shakespeare called the reversal of fortune. You have the reversal of fortune because you sit in the sanctuary with a sex partner. And because you sit in the sanctuary with a sex partner then the devil has put a muzzle on your mouth, and he's handcuffed your hands because you have the guilt and sting of sin sitting beside you. I don't want you to blow your cover, because they may be beside you right now looking over your shoulder while you're reading this book.

My last case is after I put a muzzle on his mouth, after I handcuff his hands – before I get to the third point I have to tell you that there's another dynamic because the teaching point of this principle has been "what do you do when a Hannibal's after you?" But what do you do conversely when you're Hannibal? I'm talking to a lot of sisters, because some of you just go to church to find a man. Some of you just go to collect numbers. But God said I'm about to turn your situation around. I'm about to make things different.

This is the last thing. I'm in the book of Psalm and now I'm in verse number five because verse number five gives me the last edict or the mandate as to how to handle Hannibal. After I put a muzzle on his mouth and handcuff his hands, I have a third thing to do to "Handle Hannibal" -- "For in the time of trouble, He shall hide me." What does that mean? That means that whenever it is that I start lighting up incense, start putting on some music, start dimming the lights; those are times I can't wait until Sunday to get my praise on, because by then it'll be too late. I have to learn how to praise Him in my living room because when I praise Him in my living room, God will turn that situation around. I believe that many of you know that if you learn how to praise God in the middle of your mess, the Lord will make a better way somehow!

Oft times in church we pray for the exaggerated sin, but not the subtleties of sin. So we in fact pray for deliverance for the homosexual and never say anything about the repeat offender fornicator. We'll deal with the men's issues but not deal with the spirit of lesbianism. There are church folks who are bisexual. There are many Christians who don't have a problem drinking, don't have a problem smoking, don't gamble but if God could get you past this one issue! Right now, you can't even begin to imagine God blowing your mind. Because you have what James talks about where you turn over to your sin, where you're no longer a fornicator, you become fornication. Because you don't understand that when the devil gets into your body he infuses your spirit.

There are some people who are drawn to you because they have the same spirit. You keep trying to figure out why you draw and attract the same kind of people. It's not because of what you're wearing but because your spirit has sent out a signal "this is what I'm down with."

There are some people who want to be delivered from sexual bondage. You love God, absolutely love God, know all the songs, but it's that area of your life that you're trying to get through. You want to do good, but "when I would do good, that's when they call." When I try to get my life back on track that's when I end up slipping up.

You must kill the desires of your flesh...before the desire kills you!

Scriptural References - *Psalm 27:2.* When evil men advance against me to devour my flesh, when my enemies and my foes attack me, they will stumble and fall.

LOVE ISN'T SUPPOSED TO HURT LIKE THIS!

I am intrigued to know whether it be through congress or the Constitution, how many lives have to be stolen before it's appropriate to declare war. No disrespect is intended in light of the five thousand (5,000) who were massacred on September 11th. But do understand that many of our women are under terrorist attack daily. I duly understand that they were innocent victims who did not know their culprits. But what then do we say to the countless thousands of women who are being abused by people who they raised, loved and sometimes are married to? At what point will the president hold a press conference and bring in the joint chief of staff to try to find a strategy by which we can duly and swiftly bring to an end the terrorization of black women that is taking place every day within our nation.

All of America is up in arms about what took place in New York and in Washington, D.C. But not much is being said about the abuse that is silently taking place in the suburbs of Baltimore, as well as in the inner-cities throughout this nation. Yes, I understand, that it will take billions of dollars to rebuild buildings. But how much more will it take to rebuild minds, families, communities and starving children?

If the government is not apprised of the startling statistics, then they need know that ninety-two (92%) of all violent incidents are perpetrated by men, against women. Three Fourths (¾) of women who report being raped or abused violently, say that their perpetrators are somebody with whom they are intimately involved.   Ten Thousand (10,000) women a year are killed due to domestic violence by somebody they are married to, estranged, divorced or separated from.   Forty Percent (40%) of teenage girls between the ages of fourteen (14) and Seventeen (17), can testify that they know someone personally who is abused. Whether they are slapped, punched or verbally abused, they are suffering abuse by someone whom they are involved or entranced with. Thirteen Thousand (13,000) acts of violence occur on any given work day, against women by men who they were once or are presently involved with. Eighty Four percent (84%) of those who come into the emergency room between 11PM and 4AM, are women who are there under the guise of an emergency crisis by somebody who holds a key to their home. If you don't feel that this is an emergency situation, then obviously you have slipped into a coma and are daydreaming in never never land.

But the longer we leave our women unprotected and uncovered, the longer it will take for our children to reach emotional and mental wholeness. Because most children, (eighty two percent (82%) according to a poll, who have witnessed and live through abuse of any kind, as adults, become perpetrators of that which they witnessed. And the church has remained silent for too long, when they know that violence is going on in the home of their constituents and their congregants. While women continue to come to church with sunglasses and extra coats of makeup to cover up that which they have endured all through the week, we don't remind them that "Jesus" was wounded for our transgressions. He was bruised for our inequities. And by His stripes we are healed.

At some point, as the body of Christ, we have to round up and rally and declare war on any acts of violence that are afflicted against our women and our children. To do anything less than that is counter to the cause and the will of our savior Jesus Christ. And so I talk to you today without any backing from Colin Powell or the Pentagon. But by the power of the holy ghost; declaring that the blood of Jesus will rest on every woman within our communities, who has been abused at the hands of some man even though the church has never checked them or eradicated the problem. In the same, wise brothers, the last time you abused your sister, I want to put you on notice, that day was the last day. We are now raising up a generation of black men who will not only be responsible, but will be accountable for the protection and preservation of our women and our children. This is the time.

If war is going to be declared, then we have to declare war on the enemy front that is hitting us at home. This is nothing new. But it is something that has been occurring and is as old as the bible. We find a crystal clear example in the second book of Samuel. Absalom, the son of David, had a lovely sister, named Tamar. Amnon, also the son of David loved her. Now you have to understand the problem starts right there. The problem is that Amnon is in love with his sister. And so we're not just dealing with abuse, we're dealing with incest. Incest then is a silent killer that is destroying not only our women, but our children.

The problem is further exaggerated when we find that Amnon is twenty-two (22) years of age and his sister Tamar is only fifteen (15). Now we have a similar problem right here in the city of Baltimore. There are thirteen (13) year old mothers at the Laurence Paquin School and three fourths (¾) of our teenage girls who come up pregnant, are pregnant by Negroes who are over twenty five (25) years of age, who can't handle a real woman, so that they seduce children in order to have their way. Shame on you parents who are allowing some grown knock-kneed Negro in your house to date your daughter and he can't even hold down a job. And so many of you parents are guilty culprits because he bought you a VCR and bought you a refrigerator and helped you with the rent. Later for him! Let him take care of his own mama and you raise your child. The even less addressed problem is that quite often the teenage mother is herself a victim of rape or incest. How many of you have looked at a pregnant teenager and thought, this child is bringing a baby into the world because some man she probably trusted, has violated her?

There is a problem in the second book of Samuel because an older man is seducing and infatuated with a child. But it gets even worse. Amnon was so distressed over his sister Tamar that he became sick. He became sick not just physically, but also mentally and emotionally. And sisters do not think it flattering for a man to be unable to operate in his regular faculties because he is in love with you. If it is a genuinely divine love, then it ought not make him sick. It ought to make him healthy. As a woman, you are a life giver and not a life taker. So if he is sick all the time, that ought to be the signal that you're in the wrong place at the wrong time.

He's sick in his mind, because he's lusting after a child. Any man who has sexual fantasies about a child and an adolescent is nothing more than sick. No he has not been contaminated by some video on BET. Something is wrong with his mind. And don't talk about you're just going to love him to wholeness. You better love him over to the psychiatric ward until he can get the wholeness that he needs.

In Samuel, you'll find that Amnon had a friend who's name was Jonadab, the son of Shimeah, the son of David's brother. Now Jonadab was a very crafty man. He is in fact Amnon's friend. And you have to understand that Jonadab at thirty-five (35) is giving advice to Amnon. Now put all the principal players together. At issue and the object of attention and affection is a fifteen (15) year old girl who's being lusted after by a twenty two (22) year old man; who is getting advice on the street from a thirty five (35) year old man. Now the problem with so many of our young boys is that they have been corrupted in their thinking by deranged older black men, who tell them their manhood is based on how many children you have and how many women you have blowing up your pager. That does not make you a man. But what makes you a man is when you can get to church and lift up your holy hands and say I'm yours Lord – everything I got and everything I'm not.

Amnon is messed up because he's listening to the wrong man for advice. So men, be careful who you get relationship advice from. Because sometimes your brother will get you in more trouble listening to him than where you were before you started. Every black man ought to find another saved black man who will be their counsel, their conscience, their guidance and say, "brother, don't mess up like this." What you have to do if you can't control yourself, is you have to pray to God. "God take everything away from me that is not like you." I'm so sick of black men who can't share what they're going through because they're so insecure they think it will make them look weak or make them look like less than a man. What makes you more of a man is when you understand I don't know all the answers, but I know a God who walks with me and talks with me.

This older black man Jonadab, then gives Amnon advice and counsel. This is what you do. Act like you're sick and get Tamar to bring you something to make you feel better. And when she gets there. Then you can seduce her and have your way with her. Now, you have to understand that a lot of men, sisters, will seduce you with ill intentions. They will help you not because they have a heart for you, but because they have another agenda. And then after they've accomplished their agenda, then they don't want anything else to do with you. Been there? When you first started dating, before you gave him some, he was taking you to dinner; taking you shopping; taking you on trips... . But now you have blown the whole thing!

Tamar, being a good sister, went to her brother Amnon's house. Made him something to eat (trying to take care of a brother when he's down). And once she gets there, he asks everyone else to leave the room. Once they leave, he says, "I'm not really sick. I'm really not hungry. I'm just trying to get down with you. If only for one night. I'm not going to tell anybody! This is just between me and you. We can keep it on the down low, nobody has to know. This is just between me and you." And Tamar who is a saved woman says, "brother, please don't even trip, you must not know who I am." She said, 'if you want to sleep with me, then go see the king. And the king will then release you, but you have to marry me first." Ladies, any brother that you want to be involved with, make sure they know how to talk to God. And if they don't know how to talk to God, that's the wrong one. Tell him take your Prada shoes. Take your coach bag. Take your cubic zirconium earrings and leave me with Jesus. I'll be all right.

Tamar said brother please don't do this. We're from Israel and we don't act this way. Now you have to understand that Israel is the place of God's chosen people. Now there's something that ought to differentiate people who are in the church and people who are outside of the church. And the reason that I'm addressing this subject is because the abuse that's being inflicted is not just by people who are not saved. But it's also being perpetrated by people who are saved. And I know some of you all are lying in bed next to, or are on your way home to your abuser. But you can be loosed. You can be free.

Tamar said, "don't do this. You don't understand who you are. You are a child of the king." Now do understand that Amnon is the crown prince. That means he's the oldest son. He has wealth. He has influence. And he has power. And the only thing that mattered to him at that moment was getting to that woman – his sister. And she reminded him, "you're going to blow everything because you're not being responsible to who you are." And many black men in their moments of rage and unbridled lust lose perspective of who they are and what they are called to be. There is more to you than another sexual conquest and a notch on your belt. But you have to come to your senses and say, God did not save me just for this. He saved me not to abuse women, but so that I could protect a woman. Some of you brothers better shape up or you're going to get shipped out. That's why we are losing so many black women to white men and lesbians. Because black men aren't handling their business. Yes, I said it and wrote it! At some point we have to get ourselves together.

Tamar said, "after you do this, where will I go? What will I do? You will make me lose all honor and integrity. But not only that, you will look like a fool." And the bible shares with us, that he did not listen to his sister. But he forced her to sleep with him and then he left her. Now, I'm talking and ministering to every woman reading this book, and if you know a sister who doesn't have the book, you tell her for me. (I hope you can embrace what I'm saying right now.) First I must say "it is not your fault." Then I will say, if he hit you once, he hit you too many times. I know he said "it's a mistake." Tell him "it's a mistake you're going to jail. It's a mistake you won't be around Easter. It's a mistake you won't be sitting under the Christmas tree. It's a mistake I'm not going to bail you out. It's a mistake you're going to have to go audition for "Oz." But your worst mistake is that you hit a woman whom God anointed me."

And some of you have been too passive against people who perpetrate violence in your lives. I know they're sorry. I know they didn't mean it. I know it was a mistake. But call the police. Call the police today if they did it last week call 'em. I'll loan you fifty-five cents ($.50) but that Negro has to go to jail.

Tamar says "how can you do this thing to me? You do not respect who I am. You do not respect who God called me to be." And anybody who lays their hands on you or abuses you has no sense of who you are in the kingdom of God. Because if they understood that you were a treasure in the eyesight of God, then they would treat you like a precious stone. They would cultivate you like a precious rose. They would value you like a precious diamond. You don't see nobody knocking no diamonds down the street. You better stand up for who you are. I'm not telling you to fight them, but you better find some brothers and some cousins who got your back. (Forgive me, I'm just a saved thug!)

Tamar says, "what am I going to do now that you are doing this to me?" Amnon did not listen and had his way with her. Now this is going to blow your mind. Then Amnon hated her so much that his hatred towards her surpassed the love he initially had for her. It's right there in the bible. In all reality it's not that he hated her, but he hated himself. And because he did not have enough maturity to see that he was the one that was wack, he took it out on her. So in order now to give himself some time out time, he has to find a way to release his frustration on somebody who's more vulnerable than himself. I don't care how much the man's been on his back at work. I do not care how he's been racially profiled and pulled over on the highway. It does not give him license or authority to abuse you because he has a short temper and a bad attitude. Furthermore, it's only because he did not love her that he then began to hate her. That then says that he never loved her from the beginning.

Now let me say this to you, a lot of you confuse and co-mingle lust and love. You know if a person really loves you is if they love you even if they're not sleeping with you. But if they stick by you and see that you are a virtuous woman and say they're going to hang in there anyway because they see the God that is in you, it may really be love. Amnon's hatred for Tamar exceeded his love for her.

He called to his servants and said, put her out. Put this woman out and lock the door behind her. He was trying to play her, as if she was trying to come on to him and he didn't want to be bothered. Now you do understand that Tamar is a daughter of the king. She's royalty in her own right. She's dressed in the garb of a princess. But he has them take her royal robe off of her and then they put her out on the street as if she's worthless. And a lot of men who have in fact violated you have disrobed you of your countenance, of your self-esteem and your value; to make you feel as if you're not worth anything, that you'll never go anywhere, that the only way you can survive is with them. So consequently when they beat you, they brainwash you into believing you are not worth anything. They want to break you down because they're afraid that you'll rise up! And most men who are perpetrators of violence against women are men who are insecure punks, who cannot handle a strong intelligent woman. (I'm sticking by that statement whether you like it or not.)

Amnon said lock the door behind her, because I don't want her coming in. Sometimes sisters you have to thank God for a locked door. Because even if she wanted to go back in, she couldn't go back. I know there's someone reading this book who God has locked you out of some relationship. I know you miss him or her. I know you been crying over him or her. I know you think they have good potential. But God has locked the door saying, "don't even try it." Try door number two (# 2), I have something greater for you; that you will never have to cry over.

Later, in the book of Samuel, Absalom, Tamar's brother said to her, "has Amnon your brother been with you? But now hold your peace my sister, he's your brother!" In other words, her family didn't even want her to get help. The family knew what was going on, but never stepped in to intervene. The family knew what kind of pain she had and what kind of scars she had to live with. But they never spoke out. They said "no, it will look too bad. Just hold your peace."

A lot of you, who have been going through this cycle of violence, have not been doing it alone. Your family has known, but has turned a blinded eye. And you don't know whom now to turn to, because your family is saying "it's okay. He loves the kids. He has a good job (with benefits). I don't ever remember you being this happy. Your father was the same way. You know men will be men." The devil is a liar. The generational curse has to break with you. And even if your family doesn't see that this is killing you, you better see for yourself. You don't want your children involved in this kind of foolishness.

The bible says then that Tamar lived in Absalom's house the rest of her life as a desolate creature. In other words because of the scars of her past and the affliction of her abuse, she never had a healthy relationship. She was never able to have children. She never got married. And she remained living in her parents' house, because she never got the wholeness and the healing that she needed so that she could pick herself up and try all over again.

Now I want to share this with you. Do you remember where it says when Amnon was going through lust in his body, he had a friend? For every woman who has lived through abuse. For every woman who has lived through violence. Just as your perpetrator had a friend, God has given you a friend. And the friend that God has given you is like a brother who sticks with you. He will protect you, encircle and encamp you, even when your mother and father forsake you. That's when the Lord will lift you up. And some of you all have to be honest. There were nights that you cried, and days that you had to call into work sick. But just when you didn't know how you were going to make it. Your friend named Jesus showed up and said, "I'll fight your battles for you."

If you're dealing with the scars of domestic violence, sexual or other abuse, I want you to know that you will never have to live with violence again. You will never have to run for your life. You will never have to hide for cover. You will never have to be worried about security. I've asked God to protect you from the top of your head, down to the souls of your feet. And as for your perpetrator, I'm asking God to move on them until they get saved. Move on them, until they get their lives together. Move on them until they get transformed under the anointing of the Holy Ghost. And Lord we're not going to let that situation make us bitter, but we're going to let it make us better.

Now, for the brothers who are reading this book, I know some of you are ready to be honest today. This is what you must ask of our Lord.

God I need you to deal with me. Whether it's my anger. Whether it's my temper. Whether it's my sexual proclivities. God I need you to speak to me because I don't want to go on living like this. I now recognize who I am. That I am anointed and ordained to be a son of you. And I know there is more to me than my animalistic behavior.

There is more to me than me flying off the handle. I believe
God that you are a miracle worker. That you are a healer
and that you are a deliverer.

Brothers and sisters, we have to declare war on the violence
that's affecting and afflicting our children; that's affecting our women;
and that's corroding our communities. But it's not until we get a
defender by the name of Jesus, that victory will be ours!

Scriptural References - *2 Samuel 13: 11 – 17.* But when she took it to
him to eat, he grabbed her and said, "Come to bed with me, my sister."
"Don't, my brother!" she said to him. "Don't force me. Such a thing
should not be done in Israel! Don't do this wicked thing. What about
me? Where could I get rid of my disgrace? And what about you? You
would be like one of the wicked fools in Israel. Please speak to the king;
he will not keep me from being married to you." But he refused to listen
to her, and since he was stronger than she, he raped her. Then Amnon
hated her with intense hatred. In fact, he hated her more than he loved
her. Amnon said to her, "Get up and get out!" "No!" she said to him.
"Sending me away would be a greater wrong than what you have
already done to me." But he refused to listen to her. He called his
personal servant and said, "Get this woman out of here and bolt the door
after her."

INDECENT PROPOSAL

Nelson Mandela, the former president of South Africa, was in jail for 27 years simply because he was a voice for the oppressed. What has not been widely discussed is that Nelson Mandela had several opportunities to get out of jail. They went to him on varying occasions and said "if we release you from jail you must remain silent," he refused. They went another time and said, "we're going to let you out of jail but you must leave the country," he refused. They said a third time, "we will let you out of jail but you have to go along with the system," he flatly declined.

You have to understand that Nelson Mandela was just married six months before he was incarcerated. He was a father; had a new home, a new wife, and new children whom he would have liked to have seen, but could not for the sake of his principles. It was a nice proposal to let him out of jail because he did nothing wrong but speak truth to power. But where the proposal became indecent was when they wanted to compromise his morals, his ethics, and his values.

Many of us on a daily basis are given and served proposals. What makes the proposals indecent is when they go against the will of God. There are some things that God has for you but it's a matter of how you allocate His purpose for your life that turns it into sin. God has made you and ordained you to be prosperous, but that does not give you a license to deal drugs because you were born in the hood. That makes it an indecent proposal.

And even while it is a taboo in the black church, sex is not against the will of God. There are some things that God has put in place on your body that solely fulfills a sexual function. It's just a matter of how you get that need met that takes sex from a desire to a sin. If God gave it to you He wants you to use it, but He wants you to use it based off of His will and His law. A lot of us need to understand that we have legitimate desires but have illegitimate means. Because God is not against your sexuality. It's a matter of how you perpetuate your sexuality. Your sexuality is not for you but under the ordination of what God has called for you. So, many of you who are professional fornicators need to understand that you are not operating out of practice but you are operating out of flagrant disregard of what God has for you. So that when God gives you what He has for you, you won't appreciate what He's given to you because you've already used up what He wants you to save for somebody else.

You ask, how then do I wrestle between my legitimate desires with illegitimate proposals? Because everyday there is something that wants to make my desire illegitimate when I know naturally what I feel is natural. But I went to some crazy church that tried to make me feel that I don't feel what I feel but even after I leave church I feel what I feel. And so I have to deal with what I feel. Because I don't care how much you fast, I don't care how many revivals you go to, I don't care how many times you go to "Thou Art Loosed," there's still going to be something inside of you... I have to figure out how it is that I deal with this.

While I was writing this book an instant message showed up on my computer screen saying, "Jamal, I've been enjoying reading "Sexual Healing for Spiritual Wholeness" but I think to help illuminate your idea I'd like to testify. I said, "Joseph, tell me what you have. There are people all over the world who need to be strengthened by your story." He said, "I'm going to put it down in writing and you'll be able to find it in the book of Genesis. In Genesis you're going to find out how it is saved people deal with legitimate desires in an illegitimate circumstance." I said, "Joseph, thank you for sharing it with me. I think it's going to be a benefit to the body of Christ." He said "Pastor I had some problems because I was working on my job, minding my own business, with my own vision and my own dreams. I wasn't bothering anybody. I was just trying to get my job done so I could raise up out of there. I didn't want to stay on that job a long time but there was my boss's wife, she kept looking at me. At first I thought she was just looking at me but then she started looking at me with that look and I knew that we were going to be in trouble." And then she had the nerve to step to me one day and said "Joseph, listen I know I'm married, I know I shouldn't be doing this but I only need one night. That's all I need is one night. You look good and I'm just trying to be down. I just want to know exactly where you are." And the Bible says that he was handsome and well built.

Now a lot of you have to deal with the fact that the devil tempts you with stuff that you like. And the devil knows exactly how you want him to look, how you want him or her to dress and what you want him or her to drive. That's why when some of these knuckleheads come to you saying they're your husband, you should just look at them and say "no you ain't the one." Satan knows exactly what you like. If you didn't like it – then it wouldn't be temptation.

I get so sick of folks saying "I've been saved and I've been holding myself for 30 years and I have never seen nothing that tempted me." Some of us know some stuff that when we see it, we have to fight through it! If you've never been tempted then you've never had eyes. But as long as you can see, the devil will always dangle something in your face that you will want to touch. Now I know some of you are too saved to handle this but when you've been tempted by something, it ain't enough for you to just speak to them, you also have to know who it is. And I know in a lot of churches you find folk who just up in there trying to find somebody, but God said "stop checking for a mate and check for me!"

He's handsome and he's well built. Yes, because most sisters don't want an out of shape brother. God will, in fact, send you somebody that is pleasing in your eyes. Now the old blues singer said I may not be perfect, but I'm perfect for you. There is somebody, that just being in their presence does something to you. They don't ever have to speak to you, they don't ever have to shake your hand but just to see them brings up something inside of you.

Now Joseph said, "I can't sleep with you because my master has given me everything in the house and I don't have to worry about anything but eating." In other words he's saying, "look at all that I have without sleeping with you. I have my own house, my own car, I have a closet full of clothes. I have more shoes than I can put on my feet. What makes you think that I have to sleep with you in order for me to be something?" He said "I have all of this and I did it without sleeping with you."

Now sometimes God has to wake you up because some of you are sleeping with folks that you don't love. Sleeping with folk you're not married to thinking it's going to help you get to the next level. But God is saying you must wake up and figure out how you got this far. You didn't get this far from some Negro sweating on you, you got here by lifting up the name of Jesus and understanding what He can do!

Aren't you sick of folk asking you how you have what you have? How you drive what you drive. How you live where you live? Tell them "Jesus did it for me!" They can't stand that you still look that good…, and you don't even have a job. They don't know how you come to church with no money in your bank account but you shout like you're already a millionaire.

God is observing what you will do to get ahead. Some of you will sleep with folk compromising the gifts and the blessings that God has for you. But when you are an anointed child of God, you're not going to risk 15 minutes of pleasure for eternal life. I hate to say it, but even in church, gold diggers can be found! In a lot of dating circles amongst those that are "saved" there's a greater premium placed on the material over the spiritual. So a job is greater than joy, money means more than a miracle in progress, and a car is valued over Christ. "I would rather have Jesus than silver and gold", can't be just a song, it must be a mentality.

Some of you have to put your foot down and say "baby if you want to hear me scream, then come to church!" "If you want to hear me call a name, I will never stop saying the name "Jesus!" " You have to put your foot down. "If Jesus set me free, what makes you think I want you tying me up?" "If Jesus brought me out, what makes you think I want you throwing me around?"

Joseph said "why would I do this when it would upset my master? I've gotten everything by not sleeping with you. What makes you think I'm going to sleep with you and lose everything that I have?! I have too much to lose!" If you don't plan on God blessing you anymore, it don't matter who you sleep with. But there are some of us who know that God is not through with us and we don't want to mess up with what God has for us by fooling around with someone who doesn't care about us. God has too much for us! Despite how it looks, I know many of you are excited about your future, excited about your destiny and excited about what God's plan is for you!

Joseph said "Furthermore, I can't sleep with you because you're somebody else's." The last thing I need when I'm saved is some married trifling Negro, because I believe what God has for me . . .He has for me. I don't have to share, I don't have to worry, I don't have to be a number. If I can just wait until God answers. He's given me everything but you. God said I can have everything but you. I understand what God meant, because I don't need to lease somebody else's love when He's personalized what He has for me.

And some of you don't know how to wait. You're so busy planning or plotting on somebody else's man because you can't wait for the one that God has for you. But there's somebody's saying "if I have to stay by myself. If I have to eat by myself. If I have to sleep by myself. I believe God has something for me! Some of you all don't understand that when you're saved, you have a right to be selfish. Because I understand what God has for me and because God has enough to provide one for me. I'm not jealous of what you have because what He's done for others He'll do it for me. Now some of you don't believe that. Some of you are saying, "I've been waiting a long time but I feel like this is my year. This is the year God's going to make a way. This is the year I'm going to meet my husband. This is the year I'm going to meet my wife. In order to let God know that I believe it, I'm going to shout like I believe it. I'm going to clap like I believe it. I'm going to praise Him like I believe it!"

The Bible says that Joseph said, "I can't because you don't

belong to me." It goes further to say that his boss's wife tried him every day. It's one thing to have to be tempted by somebody who lives out of town. But it's when you have to look at them everyday that it gets rough. "If they would just move. I wish they would stop coming to my church. I wish they would just quit working on the same job." But the fact that I have to see them everyday. Some of us don't have to wait until once a month, but every day we have a battle. Every day we have to fight. Everyday we got a war path.

This is what I know and some of you are going to be mad and put this book down, but I have to tell you. The Bible says in verse number 10 that Joseph refused to go to bed with her or even to be with her. In other words he said, "not only will I not sleep with you but we can't even be friends 'cause I know me and if you hang around here... I want to be friends but I just can't handle it." And some of you have to learn to be honest and say, we can't be friends!

The Bible says, not only would he not go to bed with her, but he would not be around her. You have to be at the point where you know yourself and know, there's some stuff that you can't be around. Now some of you are trying to talk yourself through it. "Oh well it's just a movie. He's just going to come by for a little while. It don't mean nothing. We're going to be alright." But you know that time is going to start ticking. So you have to make up your mind and say, "listen do me a favor and just don't call me. Just don't come around. I'm going to be all right. You don't need to check on me because I found a friend that sticks closer than a brother. I found somebody that when my mother and father forsake me that's when He stepped in." Be Honest, haven't you had to leave somebody before?! Sometimes you have to walk away from some stuff, have to walk away from some people; but God stood right there and said, "I'll never leave you or forsake you!"

Joseph walked away, he said no and his boss's wife screamed "rape!" He lost his job, it looked like his future was jeopardized, and he had to start thinking to himself "I should've just slept with her." Because it would have been easier if I would have done that. I want to be honest and forthright with you because some of you after reading this chapter are going to have to cut some folk out. In cutting them out, you're going to lose some things because they would pay for some stuff... It's not going to be easy when you're used to having somebody in the bed, and you roll over and nobody is there. When you "cut" some people out and you find that you are without, it's a difficult place to be in. It's at that point, the devil plays with your self-esteem, plays with your value and plays with your worth. You start asking yourself, "am I still desirable?" The devil will try to talk you into believing nobody wants you and nobody really wants a future with you. And the folk who you had to "cut" will start lying on you. And you will have to deal with what it is other people think. And you will have to explain what happened, to your family, because your family liked them. But they didn't know what kind of mess you had to go through dealing with them. People will want to know why they're not around anymore. They don't understand that you have to get to the next level. You're used to eating at Morton's but if you have to eat oodles of noodles it's alright. You used to go to Saks Fifth Avenue, but if you have to go to Wal-Mart you're going to be fine, because God promised you He'll never leave you or forsake you.

He had to lose something. Joseph went to jail for a crime he didn't commit but God remembered he walked away from sex for a principle. Nowhere in the Bible does it say that Joseph was a major praiser. It doesn't say that he was a charter member of the building fund. It doesn't say that he was an officer of the church. But God blessed him just because he said no to sex. And so while he's in jail, God blesses him to be vice president over the whole nation because he was faithful over his body.

Now there are some of you reading this and God is going to blow your mind just because you turned down some stuff that you could've had. Now some of you can't relate to this because you have never been there. But God is saying "you're in jail right now but in about 30 days you're going to bust out of there. You're going to bust out of your mess. You're going to bust out of your situation if you just praise me!"

I was trying to figure out in a practical way what I could relate temptation to. I didn't want it so lost in some esoterical analysis that it was not practical for our everyday life. And this is what I found out. The best correlation or connection that I can make for temptation is temptation is a telemarketer.   Temptation is like a telemarketer for several reasons.

Number one, because it always comes at a bad time. It always comes when you're doing something else. Secondly, every time you try to hang up, they'll call back. The third reason why temptation is like a telemarketer (for those of you like me who live by caller ID) is because when a telemarketer calls, you don't know where the call is coming from. It always says out of area or private number. Now some of you don't know where your temptation is being sent from but you ought to know that it's not from God. Because God will let you know if it's from Him! The last thing is, telemarketers don't know how to handle no for an answer. They'll keep calling you back. Telemarketers always make something sound better on the phone than it is in real life. Some of you have had some telemarketer relationships where they sounded good on the phone but when you got them, you were mad! This is how I found you can get rid of telemarketers. Are you ready to get rid of the mess in your life?

When the telemarketer calls, fill out the order. Tell them everything they want to hear. Before they can close the deal, they're going to ask you one question. The one question they're going to ask is "are you the decision maker for your house." And inevitably I'll say "no, you need to talk to my father." Some of you right now need to hang up on some folk and say, "if you want to get with me, you have to talk to my FATHER!"

I want to say something to you – a proposition is not ever extended unless the person who's making the proposition thinks you have some value. People who are trying to get with you know your value. The devil would not bother you if he did not think you were a threat to him. Some wack brother tries to get your number, you don't give him the time of the day and then he starts cursing you out. Saying, "You ain't nothin'!" "Well brother if I wasn't nothing, then why were you trying to talk to me?" He understands your value and I am afraid that many times the enemy knows your value before you do. It's not until your value has been compromised that you realize who you are. It's not until you walk out of a bad relationship and "find" yourself, that you realize how good you are! Even without them!

If you're dealing with temptation it's because the devil knows who you are and knows what you possess. And I would dare say those who have to fight with temptation the most have the most to offer. But when you start releasing yourself, then your value starts to diminish and you no longer think the same about yourself or what God has for you. The devil is a liar because whomever the Son has set free is free indeed.

I want to give you a decent proposal, the best offer you're going to get in your life. I want to give you an opportunity to hook up with a brother who does not just want you tonight but wants to love you for the rest of your life. I want to put you in a relationship where you'll never be abused. You'll never be underestimated. You'll never be talked down to. A relationship that will continue to build you up until you can look at Him and say "thank you."

It's an offer, you can't refuse!

Scriptural references – *Genesis 39:6-10.* So he left in Joseph's care everything he had; with Joseph in charge, he did not concern himself with anything except the food he ate. Now Joseph was well-built and handsome, and after a while his master's wife took notice of Joseph and said, "Come to bed with me!" But he refused. "With me in charge," he told her, "my master does not concern himself with anything in the house; everything he owns he has entrusted to my care. No one is greater in this house than I am. My master has withheld nothing from me except you, because you are his wife. How then could I do such a wicked thing and sin against God?" And though she spoke to Joseph day after day, he refused to go to bed with her or even be with her.

SISTERS SUPPORTING SICK BROTHERS

It's a severe state of affairs when we assess the disproportionate sickness that statistics indicate have affected our black brothers. Black men are the only community where men make less money than their female counterparts. Black men unlike any other ethnicity in the nation, have less education than their female counterparts. Black men in the continental United States of America are only six percent (6%) of the general population. And while Black men are only six percent (6%) of the general population, black men make up thirty five percent (35%) of all HIV and AIDS cases. Black men reportedly, according to the CDC in Atlanta, GA make up 67% of all strokes. Black men are twice as likely to get cancer – both prostate and lung cancer.

It has in fact duly been noted, that many of the things that afflict black men in their health are things that can in fact be detected, treated and cured, if they only get appropriate medical attention. Unfortunately, post the Tuskegee Experiment, black men have an aversion to hospitals, doctors and medical care. But it has been shown (overwhelmingly so) that the black men who are in better health have a close association with a black woman. If there is a black woman in their life, then more often than not, the black woman will indicate that there is need for health care.

You will note that this is by no means a new found phenomenon. Because when we go into the circumference of our text, in the book of John, you find a black man by the name of Lazarus who was living with two sisters. I wish this was recorded in the book of Luke rather than the book of John. You have to understand that before becoming a disciple, Luke was in fact a physician. Thus, Luke could have given us more intimate details on the sickness that was afflicting Lazarus. But because John was nothing more than a preacher, all that he could record is that Lazarus was sick and he had support from strong sisters.

Now it doesn't say whether the sickness is physical, emotional, spiritual or psychological. All that the sisters report is that he's sick. And in reading this text, there are so many sisters that are supporting sick brothers. We realize that whether the affliction is cancer, or HIV, a bad kidney or blood that is not functioning properly, you know in the intimacy of your own private space, when a brother is sick.

He is sick spiritually, because he will not come to church. He says he's doing his own thing but he never praises God. He never reads the Bible for instruction. And he has never had a disciplined prayer life. He's sick spiritually because he wants the whole house to bow down to him. But his family has never seen him bow down to God. He's sick spiritually because he can in fact spend $25 to get his car waxed. He can in fact spend $100 to go watch the Wizards play, but will become offended if he's asked to give more than $5 in the offering plate. He's absolutely sick spiritually. But not only is he sick spiritually, he's sick emotionally.

He's emotionally sick, because he has a problem with the preacher and makes that a problem with his Savior. Even more, he makes it a personal issue so that he cannot worship God because of his bias against a pastor. He's sick emotionally because he does not understand the gift that God has entrusted him with. So rather than affirming and supporting the queen that God has placed at his side; he becomes intimidated if she's making more money than he is. Forget that all the money is coming into the same house. But because he thinks that his manhood is validated by a pay check he's absolutely sick. He's absolutely emotionally sick when he abuses the woman who gave birth to his children and then says, "oh it was a mistake, I'm sorry, I will never do it again."

He's sick psychologically because he keeps talking about he cannot work for anybody, but spends all of his money on $140 tennis shoes that he will not even lace up to go get a job interview. He's absolutely sick because he keeps talking about "the man" is doing this to him. But he has to understand, he will never be "the man" until he knows the Man that died for him. Christ, the man who stood for him, while he was yet sinning. He's absolutely sick to sit in church and think about the things that God delivered him from. How it is that he was in jail? How it is that God delivered him from drugs and alcohol and a street corner? But he will sit in church and think that it is sissified to praise God. That same man will go to a basketball court or a DMX concert and scream until he loses his voice. But Michael Jordan or the Wu-Tang Clan didn't make a way for him. Still you go all out to get your concert and your sports on. And you have enough nerve to come in church with your arms folded and your legs crossed. Brother, you ain't nothing but sick sitting in church and letting your woman out praise you. You ought to in fact open your mouth and say "when I think of the goodness of Jesus and all that he has done for me, my soul cries. . ."

There are a lot of brothers who are reading this book who are on the brink of death. Who are on the brink of losing their sanity, their conscience, their dreams, their goals and their ambitions. And the only reason, (if you're honest with yourself), that you are not dead yet. The only reason why you are not in jail now. The only reason you are not nodding off on some corner from some high free-basing last night, is because some black woman shook you in your collar and said "you are created for more than this. You can be a better husband. You can be a better father. You can be a better leader!" Yet, there you are sipping on gin and juice. There you are with a beeper on your hip. There you are with a cell phone in your pocket. And you don't even know how to talk to your woman. You don't know how to talk to your children. You don't know how to speak up in your community. Brother you are sick. But if you're reading this book, you're going to get some healing. It's time we hold each other accountable. I refuse to have you read my book and be the same brother you were before you opened these pages. When you get to the end of this chapter and by the time you finish this book, you will be real.

Lazarus was sick unto death and sisters supported him. This is the first instance of how sisters support a sick brother. That is they called his name. They didn't talk about him or scandalize him or put his idiosyncrasies and business and short comings out on the Internet. They did not talk about him at choir rehearsal or talk about him in the beauty salon. But the sister said, "if I want this brother fixed, then I need to call his name to God." The bible records them as saying "Jesus come quick your brother Lazarus, who is sick, needs your immediate attention."

If you are not uncomfortable, sisters I need you to fill in the name, right here in this book, of the man you need God to change in the year 2002. God said, "if you have enough faith to call that Black man's name, then I'm on my way." Now if you don't mind him staying the same way he is, zip your lips. But if you know God can save ____ Damien ____, this year. That this is the year that ____ Damien ____ is going to be a father. This is the year that ____ Damien ____ is going to be a husband. This is the year ____ Damien ____ is going to be a leader. I dare you to take out your pen and write the name of that black man right now! You do understand that there is not any power in that man's name. So before you write that man's name (or if you already did), there's a name that you must call out loud right now. The bible says that they sent a two-way page to Jesus and said "Lord come quick!" If you need God to save a man that's in your life, you better stop calling his name, and start calling on the name of Jesus. Do you realize that "at the name of Jesus every knee must bow and every tongue must confess." "Do you know if you call on the name of Jesus, demons have to get back." They called his name and said "Lord the one you love is sick."

Within the book of John, it shares with us some insightful information about the relationship between the sisters and the brother. They categorize and define the relationship of the brother through the sister. Lazarus was the brother to the sister who had enough sense to worship God when God showed up. Now nowhere in the bible do we find that Lazarus was a worshipper. But because he was associated and connected to a woman who was a praiser, then God knew him through that woman. The praise you gave all last year in church, snotting, crying and rolling around hoping for your man to get saved, delivered and receive a breakthrough -- God said, "don't you think I was ignoring you, I was just waiting to see if you were able to hold on until 2002. Now because of the praise you gave me when he broke your heart. The praise you offered when he backslid. Because of the praise you gave me when you didn't know how you were going to raise your family -- know I am going to bless you because I'm in love with you."

There's a man in your life who's about to get blessed not

because of him but because of his relationship with you. And if he has any good sense, he's going to learn how to take care of you because your blessings are connected to him. I know I'm reaching a lot of saved sisters who are reading this book. You had a man leave you, and it wasn't until he left you that his entire life fell apart. Then he had to come back, begging, pleading and crying saying, "I don't know what's wrong, but ever sense I left you I can't get anything right." That's because he didn't know that his blessings were connected to a black woman.

Sisters, do you know that there's a blessing in your bosom and when your praises go up that's when the blessings come down? Sisters reading this book can you ask God to save that man. There's a blessing connected to you. Do you not understand that any man that gets you is blessed. They can only do better by sticking with you. Because there's a blessing in your hair, in your heart and in your praise.

The bible says that the sisters supported him by speaking up for him. Secondly the sisters supported him by expecting the best for him. The bible says that Jesus hung out where he was an additional two days, and then finally showed up. One sister ran out to meet Jesus at the state line and said, "had you been here, our brother would not have died." And I know a lot of sisters have secret prayers and secret hope for a man your family told you to give up on. You keep saying to yourself, if "I could ever get that man to church. If I could ever get him under the power of the Holy Ghost. If I could just get him into the house of the

Lord just one time, I don't know what it is, but I just feel like God could turn his situation around." So many people are expecting the worst from him. That man does not need somebody tearing him down, reminding him of all of his mistakes and all of his problems. Black women you don't even realize that when God gave you to him, he made you a prophet. So you have to prophecy into the life of that black man. Say to the brother, "I don't care how bad your day was, tomorrow's going to get better." You're going to have to prophecy into the life of that man. Tell him, "this week you're going to find a job. This week you're going to find a way to get back into school. This week your situation is going to turn around." Sisters prophecy to your man. Tell him, "it has to get better right now!"

The third way that a sister can support a brother, (and this may make some brothers upset), is there comes a point that sometimes when you're dealing with a man and he gets so sick, you have no choice but to go ahead and bury him. You just have to make up in your mind, look brother the help you need, I can't give you. In the Bible, the sisters buried the brother. They said this brother is too sick for me. In other words, some brothers (as far as you're concerned) you just have to let them die. You can't have any dealings with him. They cannot be in your space. **"NO, we cannot JUST BE FRIENDS!!!!!!!!!! No you cannot call me. No I don't need you to take me to dinner. As far as I'm concerned, you're dead."**

Inevitably, the sick brother is going to ask you, "when can I come back home? When can I call you? When can I take you out?" Tell him. "You cannot call me. You cannot come home with me. You cannot take me out, until Jesus comes, because right now your body stinks." So, sisters there's some stuff you better just walk away from until Jesus comes. When Jesus shows up, He will turn your situation around.

The bible says, Jesus showed up and said, show me where you laid him. The sisters said "Jesus there's no reason, we can't waste your time, he's just trifling. I don't even want you involved with him. By now, his situation stinks." Jesus said, "don't tell me about his condition. Just point him out to me. And let me do the work." "Are you telling me Jesus, the only thing I have to do is point to that man that's sick and you'll do the rest? Is that what you're telling me? I don't have to loan him no more money? I don't have to give him a ride? I don't' have to feel guilty about leaving him? You're telling me, all I have to do is point him out and you'll do the rest?" God said "that's all you have to do."

"Show me where you laid him. Show me where he is without a job. Show me where he is with low self-esteem. Show me where he is with drug and alcohol addiction. Show me where he is with his abusive tendencies. Show me where he is and where it was that he was creepin' with you and your best friend at the same time!. All you need to do is show me where you laid him."

This is how you know that Jesus was talking to some strong

black women because in this text He tells the women, "move the stone." There are no soldiers around, it's just Jesus and some sisters. He said, "if you want that brother healed, all I need you to do is move that stone. Move whatever you thought was the last of him, and if you move your last memory of him, then I can bring him back to life. Whatever it is that he did to you in the last dramatic episode, move it out the way." Now when you move the stone out the way, then you have to step aside and when you step aside, then Jesus starts talking and says, "black man come forth." All you have to do sister is move aside and let God do the work. And brothers, all you have to do is come forth.

The bible says that when he came forth, he had death clothes on and Jesus said to the sisters, "take those clothes off of him. Loose him and let him go." In other words, brothers, you have to find a sister that can help you take off the stuff that is weighing you down in order for you to get to the next level. Undress him from where it is he used to be, to where it is he's going. And when you take that off, replace it with the garment of praise.

<u>What can a sister do to support a sick brother?</u>

1) The first thing you can do is speak up for him.

2) The second thing you can do is expect the best for him.

3) The third thing you can do when you're dealing with a terminally sick brother is bury him.

4) And the last thing you can do for a black man (in scriptural context) is undress him.

Whatever tried to kill you last year black man failed. God saved you for a reason. God saved you for a purpose. All you have to do now is come forth. Brothers can you praise, shout and rejoice to be healed? You may not even know it, but every brother reading this book, there was a sister who prayed for you. I don't know if it was your mother, your grandmother, your aunt, your girlfriend, your neighbor, or somebody on your job. Somebody, prayed for you black man! Don't you think you got here by yourself. There are some black women behind you, who have been praying for you to get to this point. And I'm putting it on the line. If it weren't for the prayers and support of that black woman, you would be dead right now. You would be in a grave right now. But know that somebody prayed for you. Somebody had you on their mind, they took the time and be glad they prayed! Be glad, think about it and write her name right here. _____

_Krysta L. Burgess_____ prayed that I would come forth, and be the man that God destined me to be.

Scriptural references – *John 11:1-3.* Now a man named Lazarus was sick. He was from Bethany, the village of Mary and her sister Martha. This Mary, whose brother Lazarus now lay sick, was the same one who poured perfume on the Lord and wiped his feet with her hair. So the sisters sent word to Jesus, "Lord, the one you love is sick."

WALKING AWAY FROM WICKED WOMEN

My sister and I had a very intense argument about the movie "Ali" and offered very different perspectives. While my father and I were cheering about the prowess, about the strength, stamina, and courage of Muhammad Ali; my sister said that she tuned out of the movie because she could not sit comfortably with his treatment of black women. She said "it as almost as if he changed women like he changed clothes. At any light affliction or offense he saw himself walking out the door."

Now to illuminate this, you will remember the scene with his second wife, while they were in South Africa while he's preparing for his big fight. All of the sports and boxing enthusiasts voted against Muhammad Ali, because they stated that his competitor was taller, his reach was longer and his weight was bigger. That there was no way Ali would be able to survive the fight. Muhammad Ali, who believed in himself, didn't care how large the opponent was. He believed he could take victory.

His wife revealed, in a heated moment, her doubt in his skill. She said to him, "I don't want you to die in the ring." In that moment, it jarred Muhammad Ali into consciousness, that the woman who he loved, whom he supported, who bore his children, did not believe in him. That was almost a death blow, beyond anything a boxer could land. To know that the woman with whom he shared a sacred space, did not have confidence in his gift.

So many brothers out there, have not been destroyed by a racist or fascist system. Have not been killed by corrupt police officers. But their dreams have been destroyed because the woman in their life, did not believe in them. And if they had a woman who in fact was able to see beyond their foe, able to see beyond whatever it is they have to face and would in fact serve as a corner man. That even while he was up against the ropes would cheer him into believing that if he would just keep swinging, he could in fact turn the fight around.

Sisters, I don't know whether you realize it or not, but you have ungloved so many boxers who wanted to make every attempt to fight for their marriage; to fight for their children and fight for their future. But because you believed that the enemy was bigger than them. That racism was larger than them. That profiling was larger than them. You start feeding to them, there's no way they could win. You kept reminding them whenever you were in an argument, about their past; about their criminal records; about their mistakes; about their limited education; about how it is they are not well traveled; how it is they're not exposed. They then started to ask themselves, if the woman I'm with doesn't believe in me, how is it that I have a chance for victory. How is it that I can win?

You do understand that this is nothing new. For in the First book of Kings, we find a man who's saved, who is involved with an unsaved woman. She's an unsaved woman, but she comes to church. So the people in church think that she's saved. But they don't know her activity and her behavior after church is over. Church folk want to know why you're still not with her, because they only saw her in worship. But they didn't see her at work. And Elijah had a dilemma because he was raised and conditioned to always respect his queen. So whatever it is that the queen asked for, he would do and oblige because she was his queen. It didn't matter that she wasn't saved. It didn't matter that she didn't invest in him. It didn't matter that they didn't have the same values. She was still his queen. And because she was his queen, he did what he could to support her, until there was a problem. The queen (Jezebel) introduced promiscuity and brought prostitution into the temple. Elijah, who had a relationship with God, said "I cannot participate, because I understand the mandate that God has placed over my life. And so I understand that you're still a queen, but I cannot participate in an illicit sexual affair to satisfy you, when in fact it angers the God I serve."

So his queen who used to love him, now is upset with him, because he refuses to sleep with her. Now as long as he stayed involved in a sexual relationship with her, she didn't have any complaints. But as soon as he shut down the sexual relationship, she wanted to destroy his life. That says to me in 2002, that you have to be leery of those who can support you to sleep with you, but cannot support you to do what God has commanded. And many relationships have been severed and broken on the pivotal issue of sexuality. It's all right for us to tithe, for us to pray and for us to come to worship together, but as soon as you get so saved that you make up in your mind that you can't sleep with me, then we're going to have a problem. Eventually she will do everything to dismantle you. Because if you're not sleeping with me, "then I'll put it out there that you're gay. If you're not sleeping with me, .then I will salt your name and say you must be creepin' with somebody else. If you're not sleeping with me, then I'll put up an antenna of suspicion to make other people think that you're unfaithful and that you're wavering in your ways."

And Elijah says, "queen I love you, but I can't have sex with you, however, I need you to support me." The queen then makes a declaration that, "by this time tomorrow, I'm going to kill you. And I'm going to kill everything about you, because you did not do what I said, and nobody has survived my wrath."

Brothers whoever it is that you're dating, be careful if the woman you're dating 'salts' all of her ex's like she's never made any mistakes, and insists that the problem was with everybody with whom she was previously involved with and never with her. For the same way that she's scandalizing his name, when your relationship is over, that's the exact same way she's going to talk about you to the next man. That should help you understand that unleashed within this new millennium in so many of our churches is a Jezebel spirit of those who have the pretense of worship, but who have the cloak of promiscuity. So much so that you will find that a lot of unsaved men prefer to have a church woman. Those men understand that in some cases (not in all) church women make themselves the most available to sexual relationships because they come and have cataclysmic orgasms by which they outreach whatever is their sexual tension in the sanctuary because they are not in fact channeling it into the enrichment of their minds. Therefore, some of the women who claim to have the closest relationship with God in church, are those who are willing to turn you out behind closed doors. Because they are not willing to make an even level commitment about who God is.

You have to then check yourself, because what the enemy does is try to set up an open-air market of promiscuity and prostitution within the church house. That's why sisters make up in your mind that you are not coming to church to find a man. You are not coming to church to get a date. You are not coming to church to get the hook up. But, you are coming to church to have a relationship with God. For the reality is as much as you love God, you can't handle a relationship right now, because you know your sexual proclivity is in overdrive, and you're trying to get God to put on the brakes, because you know you're wheel is out of control. You should understand, I've got to check myself before I wreck myself because I know there's some stuff I cannot handle. That's why God had to cut off every level of relationship when you got saved. Because he knew that the one area that the enemy was going to try and attack you the most was in the area of your sexuality. You could walk away from Newports, you could walk away from Long Island Ice Tea. But some Saturday nights you feel, I don't want no tape, I don't want no video, I not going to watch no TBN, I need somebody here.

The man who has to walk away from a wicked woman, runs for his life. He runs for his life because he understands that he can't stay and talk to her. Because if he stays, he's going to end up sleeping with her. There are some people you know that you just cannot have diplomatic discussions with. Because you know it's just going to be a matter of time, even in the heat of an argument, that it's going to escalate to something sexual. But Elijah, who is anointed says, "I know what kind of hold this woman has on me, so what I have to do is run from her before I'm pulled back into a basic carnal relationship that I know only God can deliver me from."

And God sent me on divine assignment to tell you that at this point in your walk, "excuse me Deborah Cox, but we just can't be friends. At this place, you have to tell the person, listen, I don't want to go out to eat and I can't hang with you. No, I don't need to go to no movies. I'm fine all by myself, because I have to run from the thing that I know can weigh me down."

The problem with Elijah is that he's running and leaves his brother. In the bible some of your translations will say servant. Another translation would say armorbearer. You will understand that the problem with some men who are saved is that they don't feel comfortable talking to other men about sexual issues because society has conditioned us that your sexuality is tied to your masculinity. And so even in church men feel comfortable talking openly and flagrantly about who they're sleeping with and dealing with. Because even in church, there is an umbrella structure that if you are saved and a man, you have to be sleeping with somebody. But this man who God is trying to elevate to the next level has to walk away from his brothers. Because even his brothers would tell him "go ahead, you could do it one time, just get her off your back. If that's all it takes, I wish I had your problem." I wish you brothers would 'stop hatin'' because you have to get to a place where the walk that God has called you to, you have to do it by yourself, because most men in the church cannot help you get to the level that you're trying to get to.

While, I'm on that street, let me bowl down your alley. Sisters there are some other sisters in the sanctuary who will try and suck you into their sex traps, trying to figure out what's wrong with you. In other words don't trust people just because they're in church because it doesn't mean they're in Christ. Every person who's in church is not in Christ. You can get pregnant in church. You can get an STD in church. You can get burned in church. But you ought to make up in your mind, if I'm going to catch on fire, it's not going to be from no knock-kneed Negro, it's going to be from the Holy Ghost.

Elijah runs, he gets under a sycamore tree and he says, "I'm ready to die because I don't know how to handle my spirituality with my sexuality. And because I know that this is the one thing that's plaguing me, I'd rather die than live in temptation. So he sits under the sycamore tree and says, "God take me now, because this woman says she's going to kill me in 24 hours."

Do not let any of your ex's have the last word on your destiny. In other words, whatever it is that they speak against you ought to motivate you. If they tell you, you are never going to be anything nothing without them, you ought to start celebrating cause you made it this far without them. Everyone has an ex who tried to mess with your mind, saying "ain't nobody gon' love you like I did, ain't nobody gon' be there for you like I was." The devil is a liar. You ought to understand that God is in the bus stop business. If you miss that bus, keep waiting, another one is on the way.

Elijah's under the tree and says, "God I want to die." And God feeds him so that he can run further. Now when he wants to die, he's under a tree. But God feeds him so that he can get to the top of the mountain. The bible says that it's in a span of forty (40) days. My first point to you brothers is when you're walking away from a wicked woman, all you have to do really is bear the season, because you're going to have separation pains. You will figure out the devil will try and get you within those first seven days to make you feel like there's no way you are complete without her.

But in forty (40) days, God takes him from under a tree to the top of Mount Horeb. What does that say? When he's ready to die.

When the relationship first ends. He's at his lowest point because he's under a tree. But in forty (40) days when God gets finished with him, he's on the top of the mountain, which is his highest point.

God then is saying, "whatever relationship you are wounded from, I can in fact perform perfect healing in forty (40) days." Because God said in forty (40) days, I will take you from your lowest point, to your highest point. When I'm at my lowest point, I look my trouble in the face. But when I get to my highest point, my trouble seems small and insignificant.

If you been crying, stressed, can't even sleep, can't even eat during the day, God is saying "in forty (40) days, I'm going to change your situation around." Some of you only got twenty eight (28) days left. But by the time I get to the end of my forty (40) days, I'm going to praise GOD like never before. Now some of you are saying, "it's too long to wait forty (40) days, I'm going to shout now. Even if it's day number one and I can't see my healing, I'm going to praise Him because God's going to elevate me."

In forty (40) days, He can change your season. Your issue is how do you respond in the interim period. What are you going to do between now and the fortieth day? The bible says Elijah kept running and the more he ran, the higher he got. The further you get away from your unhealthy relationship, the higher God is going to take you. And the closer you will be to Him. You may still be recovering from a divorce or from a breakup. But God said you have to understand there's something special about a rearview mirror and God has blessed you with a saved rearview mirror. In your rearview mirror do you know what it says, "objects seem **closer** than they really are." Your problem is you keep looking back at where you came from. It looks like it's chasing you. But that's just the devil trying to trick you. God is putting space between you and your reckless relationship. You want to know why some of us are running in church, it's because we refuse to look back. The folk on your row would be shouting with you, if they knew what kind of nasty relationships you survived. What kind of abusive relationships you been through. What kind of unhealthy stuff you had to deal with. What kind of negative energy was placed in your head? You mean to tell me after you got away from them, you don't have enough sense to shout? He was beating you upside your head, and now you are sitting here. Looking back over your life, you ought to say "thank you Lord."

Elijah gets to the top of the mountain. The bible says, that he's standing on the mountain and a great wind came, but God was not in the wind. After that was a great earthquake, but God was not in the earthquake. After that came a fire, but God was not in the fire. Now you're dealing with wind, and earthquake and fire. That sounds like a storm to me. Elijah keeps looking in the wind. He keeps inspecting the earthquake. He's checking the fire. But God is not in the wind, the earthquake or the fire. All of those entities represent confusion and God is not in confusion. So even while He was not in the earthquake, the wind or the fire, know that GOD was behind it. The bible says after all that God shows up in a "still small voice." When in fact you have to abruptly leave an unhealthy relationship, expect some storms. But don't let a false prophet tell you that God brought you that storm, but know that God was behind the storm.

What do you mean? If God was behind the storm, that means whatever the storm knocked down, God was going to pick up. In other words whatever you've lost in your last relationship, you are about to get it back. If you lost your joy, your self-esteem, your drive and your dream, it wasn't anything but a storm. But aren't you glad the storm is passing over. Some of you feel lighter right now, knowing "if you never had a problem, you wouldn't know God was able to solve them." He wasn't in the storm. He was behind it. Now if He's behind it, it means God is watching it. And He comes in a "still small voice" to give a word of comfort. Some of you have been in that situation where you been in the storm; where you were crying all the time and wet every pillow in your house. But it was about 3:00AM in the morning that God whispered in your ear, "I will never leave you or forsake you." It was in "a still small voice" even while you were driving to church with tears running down your face, He said, "I'm a friend that sticks closer than any brother." When you thought about throwing in the towel and thought you were useless and worthless. He said, "in the time of trouble, I shall be able to hide you." And most times when you hear God's voice, it's not during the sermon. It's not during the praise team.

It's not during the announcements. But you hear a voice when you are all by yourself, and you have to check to make sure you're not going crazy. Because you hear God speaking to you saying, "I'll walk with you and I'll talk with you . . ."

Elijah goes to God on that mountain and says, "God I'm anxious for you, but I'm the only one left. I'm the only man who does not have to question his manhood, because he's abstaining. I'm the only man who's made up in his mind, if I have to walk away from a relationship to get with you, I will be all right. I'm the only man who made up in his mind, that just because I'm not sexually active, doesn't mean I'm effeminate. I'm the only man, the only one left." And God had to say to him, "don't get beside yourself. How do you sound saying you are the only one left and you are talking to me? It doesn't make logical sense. If you're the only thing left standing, how in the world do you have me?" In other words, you are not by yourself when you have Him. And some of you insult God when you keep talking about you're lonely and saved. Because God said, "what do you think I'm here for? I'm here putting you to bed at night. I'm here waking you up in the morning. I'm here making a way out of no way and you're going to say you're by yourself."

The thing that I like about Elijah is he says, "I will leave the queen. Because more important than the queen is that I have a relationship with the King. So if the queen doesn't want me any more it's all right. She's scandalizing my name, playing on my phone, talking about me to my family. But that's okay, because I'm not in it for the queen. I'm in it for a relationship with the King. The queen is only royalty by association of marriage. The King is in his place because of natural birth right." So Elijah made up in his mind, "it's no reason for me to try to appease a substitute when I have a relationship with the original." That says to me this. In order for you to survive your sanity, your spirituality and your sexuality in 2002, you can no longer try to please people more than you try to please the Savior. If they get mad with you, if they want to quit you, if they cut you back; it don't matter because you made up in your mind, "I was living before I met you. Now the only way you can live after them is to have a relationship with God."

Elijah walks away from a wicked woman and it's not until he walks away from a wicked woman that he experiences wholeness. And I want to help the sisters. Sisters, please know this. It's a lie that it's just women that are needy. Because there are some men who are still in a relationship that they know has expired; that they know is unhealthy; that they know they do not want to invest anything in. But because they would rather be with somebody who does not encourage them and challenge them, than be by themselves. They will stay; be miserable; and end up creepin'.

If you are that unhappy that you have to keep three and four on the side, then just leave!

Scriptural references – *1 Kings 19:1-3*.   Now Ahab told Jezebel everything Elijah had done and how he had killed all the prophets with the sword. So Jezebel sent a messenger to Elijah to say, "May the gods deal with me, be it ever so severely, if by this time tomorrow I do not make your life like that of one of them. Elijah was afraid and ran for his life. When he came to Beersheba in Judah, he left his servant there.

STOP CREEPIN'

There are some of you who need to understand why you are afflicted by an oppression caused by other people. Many of us, in fact, most of us are not wrestling with controlled substances or drug abuse or alcohol addiction. But many of us need to be forthright and be honest that many of the things that keep us oppressed and stressed are not inanimate objects, but Negroes.

The reason that you have given them that much power and influence over your life is because you did not understand the first chapter in the book of Genesis. That God will in fact let you be oppressed and abused by people, when you do not assume your rightful place and authority.

The Bible shares with us insightfully so that GOD gives human beings the power over anything that creeps. Signifying, sagaciously so in the first two clauses, that the birds of the air who have free reign shall be under your subjection, even though you can't fly. God says then that you shall have power over fish, even though you can't breathe under water. Now God did not say that you'll have power over the things that live under the earth. Because God understood, that the devil is something that must be handled by God. Therefore, the things that creep on the ground are the things that you shall have power over. Now lest I take this out of context, you need to understand that you may be amongst the huge number of saved creepers!

The devil, when he came to tempt Eve was subjugated to crawl on his belly even though at one point he was able to stand flat-footed as the music minister. Music is one of the solo tools of the enemy. Be careful of those who play music to set the mood. Before the CD is over the devil has you under (under the blankets, sheets, and sometimes under the bed). But because he became convoluted within his own mind and began to believe that the praise was directed towards him, God had to knock him off of his feet and make him crawl.

Now the reason that some of you are crawling, is because you never lived right. Because you weren't living right, God had to pull the bottom out from under you. Because He really didn't care what you did in Love Fellowship. He wanted to know what you did when you got home. He wanted to know why it is that people in your building don't know you're saved. People on your job don't know you're anointed. And God said, "listen, if you are going to creep, let me take your legs off of you. Because I'm tired of you coming in church one way and then perpetrating the fraud when you get around your friends."

And I know that there are some creepers in churches who are ghetto fabulous and high saddity and stand-offish . But there are some of us who understand "I been through too much to be cute and be noticed. I go to church because I can't trip off of where I am because I remember where I been." Now some of you have not been through anything and that's why you're reading this with the utmost skepticism. But some of us don't need a praise team, we just need a memory.

The devil was in fact knocked off of his feet and made to crawl. And I would dare suggest to some of you that sometimes, it is God that knocks you off of your feet. Sometimes God has to move stuff from you because you think you're standing on your own will, and on your own power. Some of you are saved and broke. Some of you are saved and lonely. Some of you are saved and depressed. Some of you are saved and sleepless, because God had to knock the feet off of you to see how you would act when you don't have anything to stand on.

But then there's some of you who can say I don't have $5 to rub together. I don't have a job to go to on Tuesday. I don't have a car, I had to catch the subway. But I have one thing to stand on. He promised never to leave me. You have to understand, there's something about crawling that puts you in a place where all you can see is the ground. I don't know if you've ever lived in a place where you are just eatin' dirt because you're that close to the ground. You're hanging around people who you know don't like you. But you hang around them anyway. You're eatin' dirt. You're staying with a Negro who you know is lying to you. But you stay in it anyway. You keep living in a place when you know you should be further along. You keep compromising your intellect, your gifts and your talents to make mediocre Negroes feel comfortable. What is that? Eatin' dirt. But God said I did not ordain or anoint you to be in the dirt, you better lift up your head and see who you are.

I want to illuminate for you the creepin' things that the devil underestimated. Because some of you have been down so long that as the blues singers say "gettin' up ain't even on your mind." But God is going to change your direction. You have to understand that the devil meant it for evil. But God meant it for good. Now what you must understand is that the "devil" in the Grecian translation means the "author of confusion." But what the devil did not calculate or understand is that the Lord knows how to mess the devil up. And the way to mess the devil up is to flip the script! And to confuse the confuser.

Some of you who have been eating dirt at your bottom level for a long time. You ain't never lived this bad before. But I stopped by to tell somebody on this divine assignment, "hold on."

The reason you had to wait is because God wanted to see whether you could survive the rough spots. But He's about to turn it around. Your finances are about to change. Your relationship is about to change. Your job is about to change.

You have to understand that this is how the enemy got confused. He got confused because when he saw you creepin' around, he thought that you were a worm. Now a worm has a very short lifespan and is just used as bait to catch something else. Now, some of you have been used as bait by the enemy to try to steal your praise. To steal your sanity and to steal your Christianity. That's because the enemy under-calculated and wrongly dissected who you were. He thought because you were a creepin' thing you were a worm. But when you look through the anointed lens, you're not a worm, you're just a caterpillar. There's something between a worm and a caterpillar. A worm is born a worm, but dies a Butterfly.

Because God ordained you as a caterpillar, God knew that there would just be a finite time that you would be on the ground eating dirt as the scum of the earth. When God saved you, you were predestined to change. And when God changed your future, God put something inside of you that was going to change your destiny.

Now a caterpillar is different from any other creeping thing. It has the strange gift to spew out of its mouth a tangible substance that births what's known in geographical terms as a cocoon. You then have to understand that a cocoon is spewed out of the mouth of the caterpillar and then covers the caterpillar's full body. Many of you don't understand that what happens in the cocoon is the birthing process. It is the process where you're transitioning from a creeping thing to a flying thing! Now, when you're in a cocoon, nobody on the outside can see what's happening on the inside.

If you're reading these words, you have to understand that when He puts you in a cocoon, God isolates you and puts you into exile so that nobody can mess with the process, the plan or the program. Now you know you are about to change when you been left by yourself. When nobody is there to help you get to the next level! And I know somebody reading this book just got dumped or just found themselves with no friends. But God sent me to let you know, honey you ain't by

yourself. You are just in the cocoon.

While you're in the cocoon, nobody can see in and you can't see out. Sometimes your future looks so bleak that it doesn't even look to you that your situation is gonna change. But that's just the place where God wants to get you. When it looks like stuff isn't going to get better. When it looks like your job promotion isn't coming. When it looks like you are never going to get out of that hooptie. That's when God has your undivided attention.

Many people haven't figured out how to read the signs to know when stuff is going to change. They don't know how they're going to get out of their mess. They don't know how they're going to pay their bills. But I heard the singer say, "don't wait til the battle is over, you can shout right now." Am I talking to you when I say, you don't know how you're going to pay your rent, don't know how you going to pay the phone bill, don't know how you going to go back to school next semester? While you're in your cocoon, you have to say to yourself, there's a bright side somewhere.

In the cocoon, you have to understand that no substances can come in. So what I have to consider is how does the caterpillar eat? If he's evolving and growing, how does he eat in order to get to the next level? It dropped in my spirit that sometimes a caterpillar has to eat its own mess to get strength for survival. This is a great example of how your strength is made perfect in weakness. That stuff you went through a few months ago. The pain you felt during the holidays. The set back you endured last summer. God is saying, if you'll just eat dirt' a little while longer, I'm giving you a brand new menu.

But some of you are not ready to get to the next level. You are not ready to get to the next place in God. That's why you are questioning everything I say with sheer skepticism. But there's some of us who are saying, "God I'll take it. I'll eat the mess, I'll eat the sorrow, I'll eat the set back, because I trust that you may not come when I want you, but you're always right on time!"

Now, there is not in any cocoon, a pager. There's not in the cocoon a Franklin Planner. No. There's not a Motorola Two Way. So how does the caterpillar know when it's time to get out? He knows when he begins to be too big for his problem! Some of you have outgrown your mess and the stuff that would have held you captive last year, is nothing this year. You have to learn when it's time for you to fight. But some of you are comfortable in your cocoon and are not ready to get out. But I think many more of you are ready to bust loose from everything that has had you tied up. But you have to understand in order for you to bust loose, you have to start moving your hands.

That then says to me that the only folk who get out of their cocoon are praisers! Because the folk who are sitting there with their arms folded and their legs crossed are not moving. But whenever you're lifting up holy hands and begin to praise God, that says to God, "I'm ready to come out of whatever I'm trapped in."

You have to understand then, that when you're wrapped up, the only way that you can get out off the cocoon is to start moving. Now, I might have to say to some of you who are stuck up, that you're going be unnerved. Because your brother or sister who's also reading this book may feel like bustin' loose. They feel like gettin' out off the mess that they're in. They refuse to be tied up and bound by what the enemy said that they were.

Now I don't know how tight your cocoon is wrapped around you, but your praise is indicative and reflective of how much you want to get out of there. If you don't mind staying depressed, staying with low self-esteem, continuing to fight with your family, stay in your cocoon! But for those of you, who feel like breakin' out of poverty, breaking out of unemployment, breaking out of low self-esteem; you need to know that the cocoon is squeezing you and it's time to come out.

Those who feel like gettin' to the next level, you have to praise Him, like you gettin' out of something. Now some of you are not convinced and you're praising because you think you're doing your pastor, your mama or your grandmama a favor. But those of you who have to fight to survive, fight to win, fight to get out of your mess, I need you to praise God like there's a gun to your head that is cocked and loaded. Like God is asking you, "do you wanna get out tonight? Do you wanna be released? You wanna be set free?" I dare those who are desperate to get your praise on. Come on fight your way out, scream your way out, lift your way out, rejoice your way out, jump your way out.

A caterpillar in a cocoon changes its identity. Because a butterfly is not given the surname – formerly known as caterpillar. In other words when God changes you, you are no longer identified as what you used to be! Some of you missed that. Let me break that down. As a matter of fact, when the change comes, you no longer even look the same. In that cocoon you get a full makeover. You will no longer look the way you used to look. You will no longer talk the way you used to talk. You will no longer be as broke as you used to be. You will no longer be as lonely as you used to be because God has changed your identity.

The deadliest thing, the most unthinkable thing that you can do to a caterpillar when they are in a cocoon is open it for them. Because the breaking process of the cocoon, gives muscles to the wings. In others words, if you open the cocoon for the caterpillar, when it becomes a butterfly, the wings won't have any muscles. And so when it attempts to fly, it will not be able to get up in the air. The reason it will not be able to get through the air, is because the wings were not developed in the gym. The mess you're in right now is just calisthenics to strengthen your wings. And the reason why you can't get any help is because God has to develop your spiritual muscles during the process.

The reason why nobody can help you get out of the cocoon is because God wants to make sure nobody takes credit for where you're going. In other words, the place God is taking you next month, your mama didn't do it for you. You didn't get the hook up downtown.

Nobody wrote you a letter of recommendation. But Jesus said "I am the one who stood there."

Breaking the cocoon is then a personal, lonely process that nobody can do for you – but you. The reason I have developed from a creeping thing to a flying thing, is because when I was creeping, people had power over me. But the place where God is about to elevate me, I'm going to soar right over them. Everybody who lied on you. Everybody who manipulated you. Everybody who dragged your name through the mud. God said, "hold on, in a minute they're going to have to look up to you." You been oppressed so long you didn't even realize you were in bondage. You dress to make them happy. You wear your hair for their approval. You call at the regulated time to check in. You're under somebody else's rulership. Seek ye first the Kingdom of God and all other things shall be added unto you.

Nowhere, does it say that the caterpillar took flying lessons. There was no home video for six (6) weeks of instructional training. But God put something in the caterpillar and in you. So that when God releases you into your destiny, you are going to act like you were born to be there. And some people will think you are acting brand new and you have switched up and changed on them. Say "honey naw, I've just been waiting to fly. I've been waiting to live in my prosperity. I've been waiting to live in my season. I've been waiting."

People are not going to get off of you. Hear me. People are not going to get off of you. People are not going to get off of you until you're over them. They are not going to respect you, until GOD puts you in a place of authority where they have to look up to you for help, assistance and guidance.

For all of you who have been crawling all of this new millennium, I want you to put in your mind every person this year who lied on you; every person this year who took you through mess; every person who caused you to have at least one sleepless night. You remember the last time you saw them all you could see was their footprint because they were stepping all over you. But now I'm going to make you change your location so that all you can see is the top of their head, because you are about to fly over them.

I know many of you are saying, "I don't believe you. I've read Genesis so many times, I can't see where this is scripturally substantiated. You have to help me then understand how it is that I can get to this place. Because I been creeping so long and I'm not used to flying. Where is there a biblical basis that supports you? Theoretically how can it be that the caterpillar is in itself, where I am? And the butterfly is where I'm going?"

If you haven't day dreamed on me, you understand that before you were a butterfly, you had to crawl. And while you were crawling you were eating dirt and were treated like the scum of the earth. Now in order for you to become the butterfly, there is an interim position called the cocoon. "But what do I do in between the era from being a caterpillar to becoming a butterfly? How then do I not give up on God and the gift that He's putting in me?" Well I'm glad you asked. I stopped by Isaiah the other day and Isaiah told me, "they that were caterpillars who waited on the LORD shall renew their strength. They shall mount up on wings like eagles. They shall run and not faint. They shall walk and not get weary."

My brothers and sisters, with the power vested in me, in the name of the Father, in the name of the Son, in the name of the Holy Ghost, I now pronounce you a butterfly.

You will no longer crawl. You will no longer be the last, but you shall from this moment forward, be the first of what God has for you. If you claim to be a butterfly, spread your wings and fly above your mess. Fly! Fly! Fly! Fly!

Repeat out loud: *Lord, I'm coming to you, believing your word, that he who the son sets free is free indeed. God I know that you anointed me to be a butterfly. I know you did not save me to eat dirt. I know you did not pick me to be at the bottom. So right now. I'm begging you to release me from the bondage of (insert the person's name).* Damien A.K. Hartwell *I dare you to write the person's name. In the name of Jesus, I want to be free of* Damien A.K. Hartwell *. I want be live without* Damien A.K. Hartwell *from this moment forward and I claim it done!*

Scriptural references – *Genesis 1:26.* Then God said, "Let us make man in our image, in our likeness, and let them rule over the fish of the sea and the birds of the air, over the livestock, over all the earth, and over all the creatures that move along the ground."